NATIONAL
GEOGRAPHIC
KiDS

D0132079

BOOK OF
HOW
THINGS
WORK

AMY SHIELDS

NATIONAL GEOGRAPHIC
WASHINGTON, D.C.

HOW DOES WATER TURN TO ICE?

Water turns to ice when it loses heat. Cold air pulls heat out of water. The temperature has to be **32 degrees Fahrenheit** (0 degrees Celsius) to make water begin to freeze.

FROZEN WATER is lighter than liquid water. That's why ice cubes float.

All living things need water. The planet needs water. Do what you can to save water and keep it clean.

2

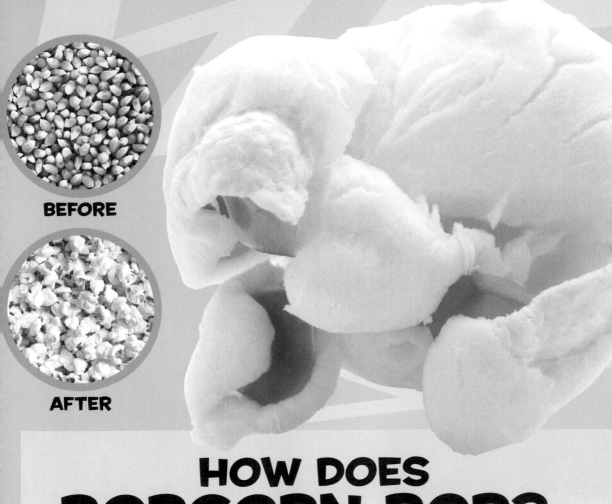

BEFORE

AFTER

HOW DOES POPCORN POP?

Every corn cob is covered with seeds. They are called kernels. Popcorn kernels are wrapped in a watertight shell. The seed is inside, with a little bit of water. **When a popcorn kernel is heated, the water inside turns to steam.** The steam creates pressure within the kernel, causing it to burst. It's an explosion strong enough to turn the seed inside out, making popcorn.

HOW DOES THE DOCTOR KNOW I'M HEALTHY?

Doctors use their senses to help people. They look, listen, and touch. A healthy throat is pink and wet. Red splotches, white dots, swollen tonsils, or an infected **uvula** (that little dangly thing) are all signs that can tell a doctor if you are sick.

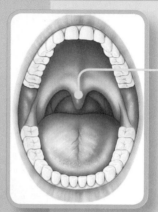

? What does a **UVULA** do? Some doctors don't think it does anything. What do you think of that?

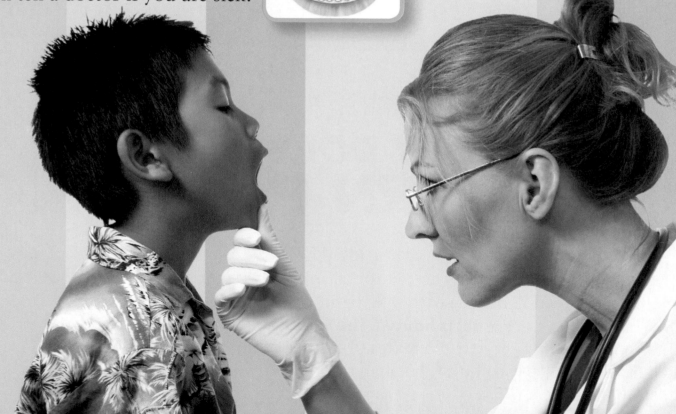

LISTEN-IN EXPERIMENT

Listening to your body is a way of making sure it's working right.

YOU'LL NEED

1- to 2-foot (30-60 centimeter) length of plastic tubing

2 funnels

Doctors say a beating **HEART SOUNDS** like *lub-dub*. What do you think?

1 Place the funnels in each end of the tubing. If it's a tight fit, heat the ends of the tubing with a hair dryer to make it stretch.

2 Put one funnel to your ear and the other over your heart, just above your left breast.

3 Do 20 jumping jacks and listen again. How is it different?

4 Try listening to your stomach. Does it sound different before you eat and after you eat?

5

HOW DO PLANES FLY?

Airplanes have really big engines, and that's one thing that helps them fly. But it's really all about air. Try throwing a piece of paper. It doesn't go very far. Fold that paper into an airplane with wings and it will soar. The air works on the wings of your paper airplane just like it does a real plane. The air below the wings pushes up harder than the air flowing over the top of the wing. Hold your hand out the car window sometime and experiment. If your hand is tipped just right it will *vroom* up. **Airplane wings are tipped just right for flying.**

Air works on the wings of a paper airplane just like it does on a real plane.

? **HOW FAR** can your paper airplane fly?

A **747 AIRPLANE** carries 400 people and weighs almost a million pounds (453 t).

A girl in England named Mary Anning was 12 years old when she found **HER FIRST DINOSAUR.**

In 1995 a 14-year-old boy named Wes discovered a birdlike dinosaur. It was named **BAMBIRAPTOR,** after the Disney character Bambi. It is only two and a half feet (76 cm) long.

FACTS

People did not live at the same time as dinosaurs.

Some dinosaurs made nests and laid eggs.

Some dinosaurs made whistling and clacking sounds.

Some dinosaurs could fly and some could swim.

Most dinosaurs lived to be more than a hundred years old.

HOW DO DINOSAUR
BONES BECOME FOSSILS?

Dinosaurs went extinct, or died out, long ago. But their bones are still being found. **These bones have become fossils.** How do bones become fossils? First the dinosaur had to die in sand or mud, so it would get covered over and preserved. Over a very, very long time the ground became rock, and the bones became fossils.

Dragonfly

Jellyfish

Horseshoe crabs, jellyfish, and dragonflies are some animals that lived with dinosaurs.

Horseshoe crab

HOW DO BALLOONS FLOAT?

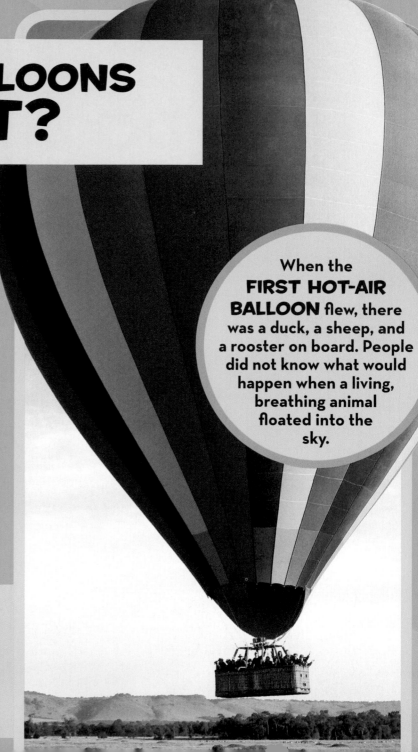

Floating balloons are filled with helium. **Helium is a gas that is lighter than air.** Because it is lighter, gravity has less pull on it, and it floats. If you let go of a helium balloon, it could go up for 4 miles (6.4 km) before it pops.

TRY THIS.

Pour some water into a glass. Then pour in some cooking oil. Oil is lighter than water. It will float on the water. If oil was lighter than air, it would float out of the glass and keep going up.

Hot-air balloons are filled with hot air, heated by propane. Hot air is lighter than cold air, so when the air outside a balloon is colder than the inside, it floats.

When the **FIRST HOT-AIR BALLOON** flew, there was a duck, a sheep, and a rooster on board. People did not know what would happen when a living, breathing animal floated into the sky.

HOW ARE SOME BUILDINGS SO TALL?

About 130 years ago, some cities had no more land to build upon. There was no room to build bigger. They had to build higher. So up they went, with the help of a new invention—a safe, fast elevator. People called these new buildings skyscrapers.

The highest skyscraper is in **DUBAI**, in the United Arab Emirates. It is 2,717 feet (828 meters) high. It has 163 stories.

Philippe Petit is a high-wire artist. Some wires he walks on go from one skyscraper to another, way up high. Here he is in 1974 walking between the Twin Towers in New York City, 1,368 (417 m) feet in the air.

HOW DO IS AN ELEVATOR GO UP AND DOWN?

An elevator carries people up and down in tall buildings.

Imagine a box with a string on top. The string goes up and **over a rolling wheel above.** On the other side of the wheel, the **string is attached to a weight.** The string has to be short so when the weight is on the ground, the box is lifted up. That's the idea of an elevator.

The rolling wheel of an elevator is called a pulley. People invented pulleys thousands of years ago.

Real elevators use **strong cables** instead of string. And they have engines that move the cables, lifting and lowering the box. And they have lots of electronics to keep people safe. Don't worry. Riding an elevator is safer than walking up stairs.

Elevators only go **UP AND DOWN.** There is no side-to-side-elevator, but it is fun to think about!

HOW DO THE STAIRS ON AN ESCALATOR DISAPPEAR?

The stairs don't really disappear. The stairs are all hooked together in a loop. After your ride ends at the top, the stairs slide under a metal plate. Then, upside down, they slide back to the bottom. **The loop of stairs goes around and around.**

OTHER MOVERS ON LOOPS

Bulldozers

Bike chains

Roller coasters

? What's the same about these movers? **WHAT'S DIFFERENT?**

HOW DO BOATS FLOAT?

Boats float because as they push their weight on the water, the water pushes back. The shape of a boat helps the water push back with enough force to hold the boat up. **Next time you go for a swim,** see how your body works in water. If you lie flat on the water, it is easier to float. If you hug your knees and ball up, you will sink.

FLOAT-A-BOAT EXPERIMENT

A flat bottom gives water more to push against. Experiment with different shapes of boats.

YOU'LL NEED

Bowl of water

Play-Doh

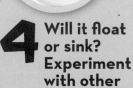

1 Make a flat-bottom boat shape with a piece of Play-Doh.

2 Place your boat on the water. Does it float?

3 Now make a round ball with a piece of Play-Doh.

4 Will it float or sink? Experiment with other shapes.

HOW DO MIRRORS WORK?

You can see yourself in anything smooth and shiny. Most mirrors are smooth pieces of glass. One side of the glass is painted with a shiny metal. The smooth glass lets light in and the shiny metal bounces it back. Mirrors show you the light from your face. Mirrors do not work in the dark.

Chimpanzees, monkeys, dolphins, and elephants **RECOGNIZE THEMSELVES** in mirrors. Dogs and cats do not.

Everyone's eyes are different. Some people need glasses to help their eyes see better. For you to see perfectly, light needs to reach one spot on the back of each eye. If your eye isn't shaped right to focus the light, lenses in glasses can be shaped to focus the light for you.

PUPILS are the part of the eye that let light in. Cats have long, straight pupils. Goats have rectangular pupils.

? **HAVE YOU EVER** looked through someone else's glasses?

HOW DO GLASSES HELP PEOPLE SEE?

HOW DOES A
TOILET WORK?

Every animal that eats, poops. Human animals too. People invented toilets so we didn't have to go outside to poop. **How do they work?** When you flush, a big gush of water whooshes into your toilet bowl. All this extra water pushes the waste into a pipe. Then the power of gravity takes the waste out of your house.

WHAT IS GRAVITY?

It pulls everything toward the ground—even your feet! **Without the force of gravity there would be no life on Earth.** Air, water, humans—everything would fly off into space. Gravity is the force within our massive planet Earth that holds our world together.

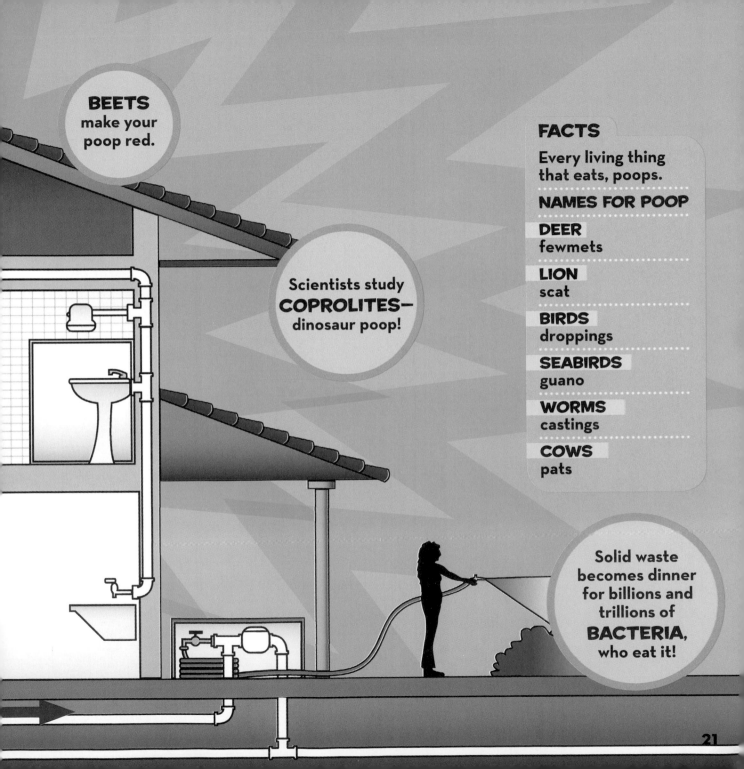

BEETS make your poop red.

Scientists study **COPROLITES**— dinosaur poop!

FACTS

Every living thing that eats, poops.

NAMES FOR POOP

DEER fewmets

LION scat

BIRDS droppings

SEABIRDS guano

WORMS castings

COWS pats

Solid waste becomes dinner for billions and trillions of **BACTERIA**, who eat it!

HOW DO FISH BREATHE UNDERWATER?

All animals need oxygen to live. Animals that breathe air have lungs that can get oxygen from air. **Fish have gills to get oxygen from water.** Fish gills have to be underwater to work. Gills are feathery, frilly, soft organs that float like waving fingers. Without water, they cannot float. They stick together. They cannot get oxygen.

This salamander has frilly ear-shaped gills on the outside of its body.

Jellyfish do not have gills. They get oxygen **THROUGH THEIR SKIN.**

The walking catfish has special gills. It can breathe in water and on land.

PARENT TIPS

BUILD A SKYSCRAPER
(Math)

The tallest skyscraper is 2,717 feet (828 meters) high (p. 11). Encourage your child to make a skyscraper from building blocks. Together, count how many blocks you can stack on top of each other before they fall over. Now try building a skyscraper two or more blocks thick. Can you build it higher?

WEATHER CHECK
(Measuring Temperature)

Water turns to ice at 32 degrees Fahrenheit (0 degrees Celsius) (p. 2). Using a weather thermometer, help your child measure the temperature of the inside of your house and compare it to the temperature outside, in the freezer, and in the fridge. Talk about hot and cold temperatures inside versus outside, winter versus summer, etc.

HOT-AIR BALLOON
(Experiment)

Hot-air balloons are filled with hot air and propane (p. 10). Help your child explore the properties of hot air by "magically" inflating a balloon. Fill a soda bottle with hot water and a bowl with cold water. Let both sit for one minute. Empty the bottle and stretch a balloon over the mouth of it. Set the bottle in the bowl of cold water and watch as the balloon "magically" inflates.

MIRROR MADNESS
(Playing with Reflections)

Mirrors reflect light and invert images (p. 18). Tell your child to write a word backward on a piece of paper and hold it up to a mirror. The word will appear normal in the mirror! Place an object between two parallel mirrors that face each other. Change the angle of the mirrors with your child to play with the reflections.

ADDITIONAL RESOURCES

WEBSITES

www.Kids.nationalgeographic.com

www.Pbskids.org

www.askkids.com

www.sciencekids.co.nz/experiments.html

www.kids-science-experiments.com/

www.tryscience.org/parents/se_1.html

BOOKS

Hughes, Catherine D. *Little Kids First Big Book of Animals*. Washington, DC: National Geographic Children's Books, 2010.

Laffron, Martine. *The Book of Why*. Abrams, 2006.

Ripley, Catherine. *Why?: The Best Ever Question and Answer Book about Nature, Science and the World Around You*. Toronto: Owlkids, 2010.

TIME for Kids BIG Book of Why: 1,001 Facts Kids Want to Know. New York: Time for Kids, 2010.

Weird but True! Washington, DC: National Geographic Children's Books, 2009.